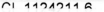

20th Century Lives

ADVENTURERS

Jane Bingham

WAYLAND

First published in 2009 by Wayland

Copyright © Wayland 2009

This paperback edition published in 2012 by Wayland

Wayland
338 Euston Road
London NW1 3BH

Wayland
Hachette Children's Books
Level 17/207 Kent Street
Sydney, NSW 2000

Designer: Jason Billin
Editor: Nicola Edwards
Picture researcher: Louise Edgeworth

British Library Cataloguing in Publication Data
Bingham, Jane.
Adventurers. -- (20th century lives)
1. Adventure and adventurers--History--20th century--Juvenile literature.
2. Adventure and adventurers--Biography--Juvenile literature.
3. Explorers--Biography--Juvenile literature.
4. Discoveries in geography--History--20th century--Juvenile literature.
I. Title II. Series
910.9'22-dc22

ISBN: 978-0-7502-6769-4

Printed in China

Wayland is a division of Hachette Children's Books, an Hachette UK Company.

Picture acknowledgements:

Cover: Rex Features; title page: RIA Novosti
Alamy: Dennis Hallinan p19, Pictorial Press p27, Adrian Arbib p29; Camera Press, London:
Gamma/1587/The Kon-Tiki Museum p15, Alvaro Canovas/Camera Press Digital p23;
Corbis: Bettmann p2, p7, p9, p12, p13 & p24, NASA/Roger Ressmeyer p5; Getty Images:
Hulton Archive p8 & p14, Paul Popper/Popperfoto p11, AFP p20, John Phillips/Time Life
Pictures p26, Ian Waldie p28; PA Photos: PA Archive p6 & p10, AP p16, Danny Lawson/PA
Archive p22; Rex Features: p18; TopFoto: RIA Novosti p1 & p21, The Granger Collection
p4, Topham Picturepoint p17 & p25.

Contents

Sir Edmund Hillary and Sherpa Tenzing on Mount Everest, several years after their historic climb to the summit. Hillary and Tenzing remained lifelong friends after their great adventure.

What is an adventurer?

On 29 May 1953, Edmund Hillary and Sherpa Tenzing reached the summit of Everest, the highest mountain in the world. It was a truly amazing achievement. They had been climbing for three months, and had risked their lives many times. At every stage of the climb, the two men had shown great courage, skill and endurance. They had also taken on an apparently impossible challenge. All these elements made them great adventurers.

Into the unknown

Adventures can take many different forms. Some explorers of the 20th century managed to reach places where people had never set foot before. Captain Robert Scott, Ernest Shackleton and Matthew Henson trekked across the empty wastes of Antarctica. Jacques Cousteau explored the mysterious ocean depths, and, in 1969, Neil Armstrong became the first man to walk on the Moon, achieving something that people had dreamt of for centuries.

Some daring adventurers have pioneered new methods of travel. Amelia Earhart, Amy Johnson and Antoine de Saint-Exupéry were all pioneers of flight. In the early years of aviation, they risked their lives to pilot tiny planes across oceans and deserts. In 1961 Yuri Gagarin was launched into a totally new environment when he became the first person in space.

Challenges and discoveries

Adventurers often set themselves new challenges, to test their skills and endurance to the limit. Francis Chichester was the first man to sail solo around the world from west to east. Ranulph Fiennes travelled around the globe from north to south, passing both the Poles and using only surface methods of transport. Miles Hilton-Barber takes on amazing challenges, such as

*Adventurers show us that anything is possible.
In 1992, the first African-American astronaut,
Dr Mae Jemison, achieved her dream of space flight.
She is shown here training for her space mission.*

running marathons over ice and through deserts, in spite of the handicap of being blind.

Adventures can often be journeys of discovery. Benedict Allen is an anthropologist who travels to remote parts of the world in order to learn more about the native people's way of life. Thor Heyerdahl made his journeys to learn about the people of the past. In the *Kon Tiki* voyage, he sailed a raft from South America to the South Pacific to test his theory about ancient settlers.

A lasting legacy

This book covers some famous adventurers of the 20th century. It also includes a few people who are less well known. All these people have inspired a new generation of adventurers. They have also shown us that it is possible to achieve a dream.

"Technique and ability alone do not get you to the top; it is the willpower that is the most important. This willpower you cannot buy with money or be given by others… it rises from your heart."

Junko Tabei in 1975, after becoming first woman to climb Everest

5

Robert Scott

British Polar Explorer

"We are very near the end, but have not and will not lose our good cheer."

Robert Scott

Captain Robert Scott led the first British expedition to the South Pole, but he died on the trek back to base. He became a hero for the British people.

Early years
Scott was the oldest boy in a family of five children. His father ran a brewery in Plymouth, Devon, and Scott grew up by the sea. At the age of 13, Scott joined the navy. Two years later, in 1883, he began serving as an officer on ocean-going ships.

Exploring Antarctica
In 1901, aged 33, Scott became the leader of the British Antarctic Expedition. Scott had to navigate his ship through icebergs and lead his men for miles over the ice, pulling heavy sledges. The team reached a point about 500 miles from the South Pole, further south than anyone had ever gone before, and also carried out some important scientific surveys. Scott returned home in 1904 to a hero's welcome.

Race to the Pole
In 1910, Scott set off for his second Antarctic expedition, with the aim of reaching the South

Name Robert Falcon Scott
Known as Captain Scott or Scott of the Antarctic
Born 6 June 1868 in Plymouth, UK
Died 29 March 1912 in Antarctica
Personal life He was married and had one son.
Surprising fact Scott's wife, Kathleen Bruce, was a sculptor who had studied with Rodin and was a friend of Picasso.

Pole. When he arrived in Australia, on his way to Antarctica, he learnt that the Norwegian explorer, Roald Amundsen, had the same goal. Scott's journey became a race to the Pole.

In November 1911, Scott began to lead his team across the ice, using motor sledges, ponies and dogs. However, the sledges and ponies could not cope with the ice, and by mid-December the dogs had turned back too. In January 1912, only five men remained in the team, dragging their sleds across the ice.

Captain Scott and his team at the South Pole on 17 January 1912. The team members are, from left to right: Titus Oates, Henry Bowers, Robert Scott, Edward Wilson, and Edgar Evans. All of them died on the trek back from the Pole.

A terrible end

On 17 January 1912, Scott's team finally reached the South Pole, only to discover that Amundsen had got there first. Bitterly disappointed, they began the 800-mile trudge back to base. By March, two men had died, including Captain Titus Oates who walked away from camp to die alone in the snow. Scott wrote in his diary that Oates' last words were, "I am just going outside and may be some time."

After walking for another 20 miles, Scott and the other two men made their last camp. All three explorers died in their tents from a combination of exhaustion, hunger and frostbite. Scott left a diary, describing the expedition and the misery of the men's last days.

Twentieth-century legacy

Scott provided an outstanding example of courage and endurance. In the early 20th century he was seen as a great British hero, although it was later recognized that he had made some serious mistakes in his expeditions. Scott inspired a younger generation of polar explorers, especially Sir Ranulph Fiennes.

Amelia Earhart

American Aviator

> "Adventure is worthwhile in itself."
>
> *Amelia Earhart*

Amelia Earhart believed that women were equal to men in "intelligence, speed, coolness and willpower". She was the first woman to fly solo across the Atlantic Ocean. Her mysterious disappearance on a flight over the Pacific Ocean added to her fame.

Early challenges

Amelia was the eldest of two daughters. When she was growing up, her family moved around a lot, and she attended several different schools. In 1917, she decided to train as a nurse in Canada, and cared for soldiers wounded in World War I. When the war ended, in 1918, she taught English to immigrant children in Boston, USA.

Starting to fly

In 1920, Amelia took a plane ride and decided she must learn to fly. She made her first solo flight in 1921 and, by the following year, she had saved enough money to buy a plane of her own. In 1922, Earhart flew her biplane to a height of 14,000 feet (4,300 m), setting a world record for female pilots.

Flying career

In 1928, Amelia became the first woman to fly across the Atlantic as a passenger. It was an exciting experience, but she really wanted to fly the plane herself. On 20 May 1932, aged 34, she

Name Amelia Mary Earhart

Born 24 July 1897 in Atchison, Kansas, USA

Died On 2 July 1937 Amelia went missing over the Pacific Oean. She was declared dead on 5 January 1939.

Personal life She was married to the publisher George Putnam, and had two stepsons.

Surprising fact When Amelia disappeared some people thought she had had been captured by the Japanese because she was an American spy.

Amelia Earhart in the cockpit of her plane. This photograph was taken in 1931, one year before her record-breaking solo flight across the Atlantic Ocean.

took off from Newfoundland to fly solo across the Atlantic, arriving in Northern Ireland 14 hours and 56 minutes later. In 1935, Amelia became the first pilot to make the difficult flight from Hawaii to California. Between the years 1930 and 1935, she set many women's speed and distance aviation records. She also wrote some best-selling books about her flying experiences.

The lady vanishes

In June 1937, Amelia prepared to fly all the way round the world. With her navigator, Fred Noonan, she flew from Florida to South America, then on to Africa and Australia. On 2 July, Amelia took off from New Guinea and headed for Howland Island, in the Pacific Ocean. During the flight, the U.S. Coast Guard lost radio contact with her. She was never seen again and no trace of her plane was ever found. There were many theories to explain what might have happened to her, but the mystery of Amelia's disappearance has never been solved.

Twentieth-century legacy

At a time when girls were often told not to take risks, Amelia Earhart showed that women could achieve astonishing things, through a combination of skill and bravery. She inspired many women to achieve their goals. She also provided a great example to younger aviators, such as the British pilot Amy Johnson.

Francis Chichester

British Yachtsman and Aviator

"What I would like after four months of my own cooking is the best dinner from the best chef in the best surroundings and in the best company."

Sir Francis Chichester

Sir Francis Chichester was an expert aviator, navigator and yachtsman. He was the first person to sail solo around the world from west to east.

A difficult start

Francis Chichester was a vicar's son. He grew up in Devon and went to boarding school from the age of six to eighteen. After leaving school, he moved to New Zealand, where he lived for 10 years. He set up several businesses, including an airline, but he lost most of his money at the start of the Great Depression in the late 1920s.

Flying and navigating

In 1929, Chichester returned to England and learnt to fly. Later that year, he flew solo from Britain to New Zealand. Because his plane could not carry much fuel, he had to fix floats onto his its base so that he could land on the sea. During World War Two, Chichester moved to the UK and wrote navigation manuals for pilots. After the war he stayed on in England.

Name Sir Francis Chichester
Born 17 September 1901 in Barnstable, UK
Died 26 August 1972
Personal life He was married and had one son.
Surprising fact After World War Two, Chichester made a living for a while by buying old maps, sticking them onto boards and cutting them up to make jigsaws.

In 1958, Chichester developed a serious lung disease. Doctors recommended that he should have one of his lungs removed and said that he had only six months to live. His wife refused to let them operate, and put him on a very strict vegetarian diet. By 1960 he had recovered and was racing yachts again.

Sailing around the world

In 1960, Chichester won the first single-handed yacht race across the Atlantic Ocean. But his greatest adventure began on 27 August 1966, when he set off from Plymouth, UK, to sail alone around the world in his yacht called *Gypsy Moth IV*.

On his solo voyage Chichester crossed 28,500 miles of ocean and was entirely on his own for nine months. He was often in danger from stormy seas, especially around the Cape of Good Hope (at the tip of South America) and Cape Horn (the southernmost point of Africa). Chichester returned to Plymouth 226 days after he had set out, after making just one stop in Sydney, Australia. At the age of 65, he was the first person to sail single-handed around the world from west to east.

Arise Sir Francis!

Chichester was knighted for his achievement. For the ceremony, Queen Elizabeth II used the same sword that Queen Elizabeth I had used to knight Sir Francis Drake when he sailed around the world in 1581.

Sir Francis Chichester sails Gypsy Moth IV *away from Sydney and heads back to England, on his historic solo voyage around the world.*

Twentieth-century legacy

Francis Chichester has inspired many lone sailors. Two adventurers who followed his example are Sir Robin Knox-Johnston (who became the first person to sail single handed and non-stop around the world) and Dame Ellen MacArthur (who broke the world record in 2005 for the fastest solo circumnavigation of the globe).

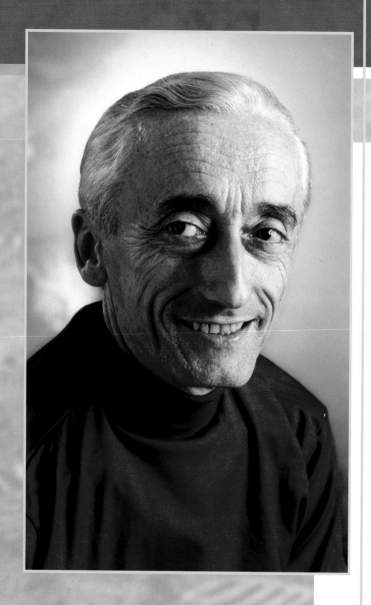

Jacques Cousteau
French Undersea Explorer

"The impossible missions are the only ones which succeed."

Jacques Cousteau

Jacques Cousteau was an undersea explorer and an ecologist. His exciting career involved scientific research, film-making and campaigning to protect the marine environment.

Discovering the sea

Cousteau spent part of his childhood close to the sea at the port of Marseilles. As a teenager he was very interested in machines and filming. He studied at a strict boarding school in Paris before training as a naval officer.

Navy work

In 1933 Cousteau joined the French navy and began to experiment with diving underwater. During World War Two, he worked as a spy and travelled to Japan and Russia. In the 1940s, he worked with a French engineer to develop the aqualung, an invention that allowed divers to stay underwater for several hours.

Exploring and filming

In 1949, Cousteau left the navy. The following year he took over a ship called *Calypso*. The ship was equipped as a research laboratory and a support base for diving and filming. For the next 20 years, Cousteau travelled the oceans in *Calypso*, studying

Name Jacques-Yves Cousteau
Known as Commander Cousteau or Captain Cousteau
Born 11 June 1910 Saint-André-de-Cubzac, Gironde, France
Died 25 June 1997
Personal life He was married twice and had three sons and a daughter.
Surprising fact When he was young Cousteau broke both his arms in a car accident. He had to swim every day to strengthen his arms, and developed a passion for the ocean.

Jacques Cousteau prepares for an underwater adventure. He is wearing a scuba diving suit, with weights around his waist, and a large air tank strapped to his back.

and filming many aspects of ocean life. In the 1950s, he discovered how porpoises communicate with each other, using echolocation (very high-pitched sounds that can travel through water).

Throughout his career, Cousteau made films and documentaries for television and wrote books, with the aim of teaching people "to protect and respect the sea". His most famous film was *The Silent World* (1956). He also made a popular television series called *The Jacques Cousteau Odyssey*.

Protecting the environment

In 1973 Cousteau founded the Cousteau Society for the Protection of Ocean Life. In the same year he explored the Antarctic Ocean in a submersible. Three years later, Cousteau uncovered the wreck of *Brittanic*, an ocean liner that had sunk in 1916. In 1977, he was awarded a United Nations International Environment Prize. In 1996, *Calypso* was rammed by a barge and sank, but it was refloated and towed back to France. Cousteau died the following year, aged 87.

Twentieth-century legacy

Cousteau introduced the general public to the undersea environment. He was one of the first creators of documentaries about the natural world and he pioneered the idea of marine conservation. He also inspired a new generation of undersea explorers, including the American scientist and diver Sylvia Earle.

Thor Heyerdahl

Norwegian Adventurer

"We seem to believe the ocean is endless... we use it like a sewer."

Thor Heyerdahl

Thor Heyerdahl was an explorer, an anthropologist and an archaeologist. He led expeditions to try to find out more about ancient peoples and their journeys. He enjoyed a life of great adventure, but was also passionate about the environment.

Early interests

Thor Heyerdahl grew up in the coastal town of Larvik. His father was a brewer and his mother ran the local museum. He was an only child, and at a young age he became interested in zoology and art. He also created his own museum with a venomous adder as the star exhibit.

After Heyerdahl left school he studied zoology and geography at Oslo University. He also became fascinated by the Polynesian islands of the South Pacific Ocean and read all he could about them. In 1936, he set off on his first expedition to the Marquesas Islands in the South Pacific. He lived for a year on the isolated island of Fatu Hiva and investigated the way that the first animals had reached the island.

Kon-Tiki expedition

Heyerdahl wanted to prove that ancient people could have travelled by raft from South America to the South Pacific islands. He built a raft from logs, called *Kon-Tiki*, and in 1947 he set off from Peru

Name Thor Heyerdahl

Born 6 October 1914 in Larvik, Norway

Died 10 April 2002

Personal life Heyerdahl was married three times and had two sons and three daughters.

Surprising fact Heyerdahl took a parrot on his *Kon-Tiki* expedition.

with four other adventurers. After a voyage of 101 days, *Kon-Tiki* arrived in the Tuamotu Islands of the South Pacific. Heyerdahl had travelled 4,300 miles. He claimed that he had proved his theory about the journeys of the very early settlers.

Thor Heyerdahl's Tigris *was built from reeds, like the ancient boats made in the Indus valley. Heyerdahl aimed to recreate the voyages of the past – and have some wonderful adventures!*

Ra and *Tigris*

In 1969 Heyerdahl built a reed boat, called *Ra*, and set off from Morocco to cross the Atlantic Ocean. His aim was to show that Ancient Egyptian sailors could have reached South America. *Ra* broke apart, but a second version, *Ra II*, reached Barbados in 1970.

Heyerdahl built another reed boat, called *Tigris*, in 1978. This time he planned to explore the trade routes of the ancient people of the Indus Valley. He sailed *Tigris* from Iraq through Pakistan and towards the Red Sea. But in April 1978 he deliberately set fire to his boat as a protest against the wars in the Middle East.

Other expeditions

In the 1980s and 1990s, Heyerdahl continued to lead expeditions to investigate ancient history. He tried to encourage better understanding between the different peoples of the world, and he was an early campaigner to save the environment. Heyerdahl wrote books and made films about his ideas and his journeys, including a famous film about the *Kon-Tiki* expedition.

Twentieth-century legacy

Heyerdahl's exciting journeys caught the public imagination. He created great interest in ancient history and in the different peoples of the world. He also challenged many theories about ancient history. However, not all his ideas have been accepted by archaeologists.

Edmund Hillary & Tenzing Norgay

Conquerors of Mount Everest

Name Sir Edmund Percival Hillary

Born 20 July 1919 in Auckland, New Zealand

Died 11 January 2008

Personal life He was married twice and had three children.

Surprising fact On the morning before he reached Everest, Hillary discovered that his boots had frozen solid outside the tent. He had to spend two hours warming them up before he could start climbing.

Name Tenzing Norgay

Known as Sherpa Tenzing

Born Late May 1914, in Nepal or Tibet

Died 9 May 1986

Personal life He was married three times and had three daughters and three sons.

Surprising fact Tenzing did not know how to use a camera so he could not take a photograph of Hillary on the summit of Everest. All the photographs show Tenzing.

"People do not decide to become extraordinary. They decide to accomplish extraordinary things."

Sir Edmund Hillary

"I have climbed my mountain, but I must still live my life."

Tenzing Norgay

Hillary and Tenzing were the first two people to reach the summit of Everest, the highest mountain on Earth, in the Himalayan Mountains of Nepal.

Edmund Hillary

Edmund Hillary grew up on the North Island of New Zealand. He began climbing on a school trip when he was 16. After studying mathematics and science at Auckland University, he became a bee-keeper, and spent the winters climbing. During World War Two, he was a navigator in the New Zealand Air Force. From 1951 to 1952, he took part in two climbing expeditions in the Himalayan Mountains.

Sherpa Tenzing

It is not certain whether Tenzing was born in Nepal or Tibet. His father was a yak herder, and Tenzing was the eleventh of 13 children. He was brought up as a Buddhist. As an adult he settled in Darjeeling in India. During the 1930s and 40s Tenzing worked as porter on mountaineering expeditions, carrying extra bags for the climbers.

Climbing Everest

In 1953 Hillary and Tenzing took part in an expedition to climb Everest. It took three months to climb from base camp to the final camp, just below the summit. Two climbers tried to reach the summit, but they had to turn back when their oxygen supply failed. Then it was Hillary and Tenzing's turn.

Hillary and Tenzing did the first part of the climb with a support team of three other mountaineers. Their final ascent involved working their way slowly up a crack in the steep mountain face. On the morning of 29 May they reached the summit, where they stayed for 15 minutes before they started the dangerous climb down.

After Everest

After climbing Everest, Hillary climbed 10 other peaks in the Himalayas. In 1958 he led the New Zealand team in the Commonwealth Trans-Arctic Expedition to the South Pole. He spent much of his life working on campaigns to help the Sherpa people of Nepal. Tenzing became director of Field Training for the Himalayan Mountaineering Institute and ran an adventure holiday company.

Hillary and Tenzing back at base camp, soon after their amazing ascent of Mount Everest on 29 May 1953.

Twentieth-century legacy

Hillary and Tenzing set an inspiring example of courage and endurance. Their amazing achievement filled many people with a sense of optimism. The example of the two climbers led other mountaineers to undertake difficult climbs, including the ascent of Mount Everest. Since Hillary and Tenzing reached the summit of Everest, climbing equipment has greatly improved and now more than 800 people have conquered the world's highest peak. However, about 180 climbers have died on its slopes.

Neil Armstrong

American Astronaut

"That's one small step for [a] man.
One giant leap for mankind."

Neil Armstrong's first words from the Moon

Neil Armstrong was the first person to set foot on the Moon. He was the commander of the American *Apollo 11* moonwalk mission.

Early years

Neil Armstrong spent his childhood in the state of Ohio. His father worked for the state government and his family lived in 20 different towns while Neil and his two sisters were growing up. In 1947 he began studying aerospace engineering at Purdue University (Indiana) but in 1949 he was called up to join the US Navy. After training as a pilot for the Fleet Air Arm Squadron, he served as a pilot in the Korean War. Armstrong left the navy in 1952 and returned to university.

Test pilot and astronaut

In 1955 Armstrong started work as a test pilot in Ohio. During the following year he moved to Edwards Air Force Base, in California, where his job involved in testing rocket planes. It was risky work and he survived several crash landings. In 1962 he was selected for astronaut training.

Gemini and *Apollo*

In 1966, Armstrong was the commander for the *Gemini 8* space mission. With the help of pilot

Name Neil Alden Armstrong

Born 5 August 1930 at Wapakoneta, Ohio, USA

Personal life He has been married twice and has two sons, and a daughter who died in 1962.

Surprising fact When Armstrong and his fellow astronauts prepared to lift off the lunar module from the Moon, they discovered that the ignition switch was broken. They had to use a pen to make the switch work so that the module could bring them back to Earth. After the safe return of *Apollo 11*, the pen was kept in a special glass case.

David Scott, he performed the first docking of two spacecraft, linking the two craft together while they were in space. In 1968, he was chosen to be the commander of the *Apollo* moonwalk mission, with Buzz Aldrin and Michael Collins as the other members of the crew.

After 18 months of training, the *Apollo 11* rocket was launched into space on 16 July 1969. Four days later, the lunar module *Eagle* landed on the surface of the Moon. In the early hours of 21 July, 1969 Armstrong took his first step onto the Moon. After 15 minutes, he was joined by Aldrin and together they planted a US flag on the Moon's surface.

As Armstrong stepped onto the Moon's surface he made his famous speech about "one giant leap for mankind". He had practised what he was going to say, but it came out slightly differently. People heard him say "That's one small step for man," instead of "one small step for a man".

After *Apollo*

Shortly after returning from the *Apollo 11* mission to the Moon, Armstrong announced that he did not plan to travel in space again. In 1971 he began a new career at the University of Cincinnati as a teacher of aerospace engineering.

Neil Armstrong took this photograph of his fellow astronaut, Buzz Aldrin, walking on the Moon. Armstrong and lunar module Eagle *are reflected in Aldrin's space helmet.*

Twentieth-century legacy

Armstrong's walk on the Moon was one of the most exciting events of the 20th century. It was something that people had dreamt about for thousands of years. He is remembered by the Armstrong crater on the Moon and there are more than a dozen schools in the USA named in his honour. After the *Apollo 11* mission, 10 more people walked on the Moon, before the last moonwalk in 1972.

Yuri Gagarin and Valentina Tereshkova are the two great heroes of the Soviet space programme.

Name Yuri Alexeyevich Gagarin
Born 9 March 1934 in Maslennikovo (now in Russia)
Died 27 March 1968
Personal life He was married.
Surprising fact Gagarin was only 1.57 metres (5ft 2in) tall. His small size was a great advantage in the cramped *Vostok* spacecraft.

Name Valentina Vladimirovna Tereshkova
Born 6 March 1937 in Yaroslav Oblast (now in Russia)
Personal life She has been married twice and has a daughter.
Surprising fact After her space flight, Valentina's face was badly bruised from a bumpy parachute landing. She had to wear heavy make-up for her press appearances.

Yuri Gagarin & Valentina Tereshkova
Soviet Cosmonauts

"Orbiting Earth in the spaceship, I saw how beautiful our planet is. People, let us preserve and increase this beauty, not destroy it!"

Yuri Gagarin

"Once you've been in space, you appreciate how small and fragile the Earth is."

Valentina Tereshkova

Yuri Gagarin was the first person in space and the first to orbit the Earth in a spacecraft. Valentina Tereshkova was the first woman in space, completing 48 orbits of the Earth.

Yuri Gagarin
Yuri Gagarin grew up in a small village in the Soviet Union. While he was in high school he learned to fly a light aircraft with his local flying club, and in 1955 he began to train as a military pilot.

In 1960 Gagarin was selected with 19 other men for the Soviet space programme. After many tests, he was chosen to be the Soviet Union's first cosmonaut. On 12 April 1961, the *Vostok 1* spacecraft was launched into space. *Vostok* competed one orbit of the Earth (taking 108 minutes) before the re-entry capsule returned to Earth. Gagarin ejected from the capsule at 7 km (23,000 ft) above the Earth and parachuted to the ground.

After he returned from his famous space flight, Gagarin worked with the Soviet space team. He advised on spaceship design and helped to train cosmonauts. He also retrained as a fighter pilot. While he was making a routine training flight, his plane crashed and he died, aged 34.

Valentina Tereshkova

Valentina Tereshkova was a country girl from a poor family. At the age of 17 she went to work in a factory. In her spare time, she learnt to parachute at a local club.

After Yuri Gagarin's space voyage in 1961, the Soviet space team was keen to send a woman into space. The female cosmonaut did not need to be a trained pilot, but the woman they selected had to have very good parachuting skills. Two women were chosen, but at the last minute, it was decided that only one should go into space.

On 16 June 1963, *Vostok 6* was launched, carrying three male cosmonauts and the 26-year-old Valentina Tereshkova. The flight was a success, although Valentina felt ill and uncomfortable during her three days in space. After her flight, she trained as a pilot and studied engineering.

Yuri Gagarin on board the spacecraft Vostok. *People all over the world admired his calmness and courage as he became the first person to travel in space.*

Twentieth-century legacy

Yuri Gagarin's achievement as the first man in space led to a series of manned space missions that still continue today. Just 23 days after Gagarin's flight, Alan Shepard became the first American in space. After Valentina Tereshkova's space flight, many more women travelled in space, including the American astronauts Dr Sally Ride and Commander Eileen Collins. In 1992 Dr Mae Jemison became the first African-American woman astronaut.

Ranulph Fiennes

British Adventurer

> "This is the closest you can get to the Moon by walking."
>
> *Ranulph Fiennes, on reaching the summit of Everest*

Sir Ranulph Fiennes has undertaken many remarkable endurance tests. He is the only person to have travelled overland to both the North and the South Poles and to have walked all the way across Antarctica.

Noble beginnings

By the time Ranulph Fiennes was born, his father had already died in World War Two. Ranulph inherited his father's title at birth, becoming the 3rd Baronet Twisleton-Wykeham-Fiennes. Soon after the war ended, in 1945, he moved with his mother to South Africa, where he stayed until he was 12. Then he returned to England to go to school at Eton College.

The adventures begin

Fiennes served in the British army for eight years, before moving to the Middle East, where he joined the army of the Sultan of Oman. In the 1960s, he decided to become an adventurer, and in 1969 he led an expedition by hovercraft up the White Nile River in Africa.

Transglobe Expedition

One of Fiennes' most famous adventures was the Transglobe Expedition (1979-1982). Using only

Name Sir Ranulph Twisleton-Wykeham-Fiennes

Known as Ranulph or Ran Fiennes

Born 7 March 1944 in Windsor, England

Personal life He has been married twice.

Surprising fact He is the third cousin of the actors Ralph and Joseph Fiennes.

surface transport, he travelled round the world from north to south, crossing both Poles. Fiennes and his companion, Charles Burton, crossed a total of 52,000 miles, and became the first people to visit both the North and the South Pole by land.

Other adventures

In 1993, Fiennes made a 90-day trek across the continent of Antartica with the adventurer Dr Mike Stroud. In 1996 and 2000 he attempted solo walks to the North and South Poles, but he did not manage to achieve these goals. On the trek to the North Pole the fingers on his left hand were very severely frostbitten.

In 2003, aged 59, Fiennes had a heart attack and had to have a major heart operation, but four months later he joined Mike Stroud in an extraordinary endurance test. The two men had to run seven marathon races (each covering 26 miles) in seven days on seven continents of the world. Fiennes completed the challenge, but said he should never have agreed to do it!

Record attempt

In 2009, at the age of 65 and in spite of his great fear of heights, Fiennes became the oldest Briton and the first British pensioner to climb Mount Everest. After reaching the summit he joked, "It's amazing where you can get with a bus pass these days." In between his adventures, Fiennes has written 13 books, both fiction and non-fiction, including a biography of Captain Robert Scott.

Sir Ranulph Fiennes demonstrates how to put up a tent on the ice. This photograph was taken in 2000, just before he set out on his solo walk to the North Pole.

Twentieth-century legacy

In his many adventures and endurance tests, Ranulph Fiennes has proved that it is possible to achieve astonishing feats. He has also raised large amounts of money for charity, by encouraging people to sponsor his adventures. Prince Charles has said of him: "My admiration for Ran is unbounded and thank God he exists. The world would be a far duller place without him."

Matthew Henson became the first African-American to explore the Arctic.

Name Matthew Alexander Henson

Born 6 August 1866 in Charles County, Maryland, USA

Died March 9 1955

Personal life He was married to an American woman, but he also had an Inuit companion who was the mother of his son.

Surprising fact Henson's Inuit son, Anauakaq, visited his father's grave in Maryland in 1987.

Matthew Henson

African-American Polar Explorer

Matthew Henson was an African-American explorer who accompanied Commander Robert Peary on his Arctic expeditions. He was probably the first explorer to reach the North Pole.

Early years

Henson grew up on a farm, but after his parents died, when he was 12, he went to sea as a cabin boy. During his time at sea, he met Commander Robert E. Peary, who was very impressed by Henson's navigating skills. In 1887 Peary invited Henson to join an expedition to Nicaragua. It was the first of many shared journeys.

Arctic adventures

Peary and Henson travelled to the Arctic several times. In the Arctic regions, they traded with the Inuit peoole and learnt how to train teams of dogs. In 1909, Henson was one of a team of six who set out to reach the North Pole. As the team approached the Pole, Henson went ahead, while Peary, who was ill, had to travel by sledge. Henson later claimed that he was the first man to reach the North Pole.

After the team returned from the Arctic, Peary was treated as a hero, but Henson was mainly ignored. He spent the next 30 years working as a clerk. However, by the end of his life, his achievements were recognized. Presidents Truman and Eisenhower honoured Henson before he died.

Ernest Shackleton

Anglo-Irish Antarctic Explorer

Ernest Shackleton was a great Antarctic explorer. He is best known as the leader of the *Endurance* expedition that aimed to cross the continent of Antarctica.

Ireland and England

Shackleton was the second of ten children. He spent his first ten years in Ireland before the family moved to London. At the age of 16 Shackleton left school and joined the British Merchant Navy.

Expeditions to Antarctica

In 1901 Shackleton volunteered to join the British Antarctic expedition led by Robert Scott, but he became ill and was sent home early. From 1907 to 1909 he led the *Nimrod* Antarctic expedition, which reached further south than anyone had ever been before. When Shackleton returned to Britain, he was knighted by King Edward VII .

After Amundsen and Scott had reached the South Pole in 1912, Shackleton aimed to cross Antarctica via the Pole. In 1914 he set sail in his ship, *Endurance*, but the ship got trapped in ice and was slowly crushed. Thanks to his calmness and good planning, no lives were lost and the expedition returned home in 1917. In 1921 Shackleton led one more expedition to Antarctica, but before he reached the ice he died of a heart attack, aged 47.

Sir Ernest Shackleton is pictured here in 1909 as leader of the Nimrod *Antarctic expedition.*

Name Sir Ernest Henry Shackleton
Born 15 February 1824 in Kilkea, County Kildare, Ireland
Died 5 January 1922 on his ship while it was moored at South Georgia Island
Personal life He was married and had two sons and a daughter.
Surprising fact When one of his crew was ill in Antarctica, Shackleton gave the man his own biscuit – his main ration of food for the day.

Antoine de Saint-Exupéry is pictured here in the cockpit of a fighter plane.

Name Antoine de Saint-Exupéry

Born 29 June 1900 in Lyon, France

Died 31 July 1944, killed in action off the French coast near Marseilles during World War Two.

Personal life He was married.

Surprising fact When Saint-Exupéry was rescued from the Sahara Desert, he told his rescuers that he and his navigator only had a thermos of sweet coffee, chocolate, and a handful of crackers. When he described the crash in *Wind, Sand and Stars* he said that all they had to eat were grapes, two oranges, and a small amount of wine.

Antoine de Saint-Exupéry
French Aviator

Antoine de Saint-Exupéry was an aviator and a writer. He wrote the famous story, *The Little Prince*, and several books about flying.

Starting to fly

Saint-Exupéry came from an aristocratic family. After leaving school, he began to study architecture, but in 1921 he was called up to for military service. He trained as a pilot and discovered that he loved to fly. In 1926 he joined the French air postal service, making regular flights from France to Africa.

Writing and flying

In 1929 Saint-Exupéry published his first book and moved to South America to run an air postal company. Two years later he had his first publishing success with *Night Flight*. In 1935 he crashed his plane in the Sahara Desert, but was rescued after four days. He wrote about this experience in *Wind, Sand and Stars*.

In 1941, Saint-Exupéry moved to North America, where he wrote *The Little Prince*. After two years, he returned to France to help the Free French in their struggle against the Nazis. His job was to spy on Nazi troops in Germany. On July 31 1944, his plane took off from Corsica and he was never seen again. Later, the remains of his plane were found in the sea close to Marseilles in southern France.

Amy Johnson

British Aviator

Amy Johnson was the first woman to fly solo from Britain to Australia. Her early death in World War Two has added to her fame.

Learning to fly

Amy Johnson grew up in Hull and studied economics at Sheffield University. While she was working as a secretary, she started to take flying lessons. In 1929 Amy gained her pilot's licence and also qualified as an Air Ministry ground engineer. The following year she bought a second-hand plane.

Breaking records

On 5 May 1930 Amy set off from Croydon airfield, in south London, to fly to Australia. Nineteeen days later she arrived in Darwin, South Australia, after flying 11,000 miles. This was the start of many flying achievements. In 1932 Amy set a new record for flying solo from London to Cape Town, South Africa. She also made record-breaking flights with her husband, the Scottish pilot Jim Mollison.

In 1940, Amy joined the Air Transport Auxiliary. Her job involved flying aircraft from their factories to Royal Air Force bases. She was flying in bad weather when her plane went off course and she crashed in the Thames Estuary. People were amazed that such an experienced pilot could get lost on a routine flight, and many theories have grown up around her death.

Amy Johnson poses for the press in the cockpit of her plane.

Name Amy Johnson

Born 1 July 1903 in Kingston upon Hull, UK

Died 5 January 1941, when her plane crashed in the Thames Estuary

Personal life She was married and divorced.

Surprising fact When Amy crashed her plane, some people suggested that she had been shot down by British anti-aircraft gunners who mistook her plane for an enemy bomber.

Miles Hilton-Barber celebrates after flying a microlight aircraft from London to Sydney in 2007. He made the trip with the help of a sighted co-pilot.

Name: Miles Hilton-Barber

Born 20 December 1948 in Salisbury, Rhodesia (now Zimbabwe)

Personal life He is married and has two daughters and a son.

Surprising fact Miles decided to become an adventurer after his older brother, Geoff, who had also gone blind, sailed solo from South Africa to Australia, using a speech-output navigation system.

Miles Hilton-Barber

British Blind Adventurer

Miles Hilton-Barber went blind when he was in his twenties, but he later became an incredibly daring adventurer. His achievements include running marathons across deserts and climbing some of the world's highest mountains.

Going blind

Miles grew up in the African country of Rhodesia (now Zimbabwe). His father was a pilot and Miles wanted to fly planes too. He joined the Rhodesian Air Force when he was 18, but he failed the eyesight test to be trained as a pilot.

When he was 21, Miles was told that he had a serious eye disease and he would go completely blind. For the following 30 years, he led a limited life as a blind person, but at the age of 50 he began a new life as an adventurer.

Amazing adventures

In 1999, Miles completed the toughest running race in the world – a 150-mile ultra-marathon through the Sahara Desert. He has also dragged a sledge for over 250 miles across Antarctica, and gone white-water rafting down the Zambezi River in Africa. With the help of a speech-output navigation system, he has piloted a microlight from London to Sydney, and set world records for a blind driver in racing cars, planes and power boats. Miles is sometimes accompanied by his friend Jonathan Cook, who acts as his guide.

Benedict Allen

British Anthropologist and Adventurer

Benedict Allen is a British explorer who likes to travel alone, learning from the local people. He has described his adventures in a series of books and documentaries.

Early adventures

Allen grew up on the Dorset coast, where he enjoyed hunting for fossils. He studied Environmental Science at university and took part in three scientific expeditions.

After these trips, Allen decided it was better to travel alone and learn from the local people. He pioneered a video diary format so that he could travel without a filming team.

Solo expeditions

In 1985, Allen made his first solo expedition, travelling to the mouth of the Amazon River in South America. This involved a 600-mile journey on foot and by dug-out canoe. In the following year, he stayed on Irian Jaya in the South Pacific Ocean. There he took part in a male initiation ceremony and was left with a chest covered with scars. This expedition was followed by trips to New Guinea, Sumatra and Peru.

In 1995 Allen crossed the Namib Desert in South Africa, learning survival skills from a nomadic tribe. Three years later, he made a five and a half month trek across the Mongolian steppes and the Gobi Desert in China.

Benedict Allen is seen here at the edge of the Gobi Desert during one of his adventures.

Name Benedict Colin Allen

Born 1 March 1960 in Macclesfield, Cheshire

Personal life He is married and has a daughter.

Surprising fact On his first solo journey, Allen was attacked by gold miners and left without any food. In the end he had to eat his own dog.

Timeline

1909 The African-American explorer Matthew Henson is probably the first man to reach the North Pole.

1912 Captain Robert Scott reaches the South Pole, and discovers that Roald Amundsen has been there first.

1914 World War One begins.

1917 Ernest Shackleton returns safely from his Antarctic journey in *Endurance*.

1918 World War One ends.

1930 Amy Johnson is the first woman to fly solo from Britain to Australia.

1932 Amelia Earhart is the first woman to fly solo across the Atlantic Ocean.

1935 Antoine de Saint-Exupéry crashes his plane in the Sahara Desert, and is rescued after four days. Later he writes about this experience in *Wind, Sand and Stars*.

1939 World War Two begins.

1945 World War Two ends.

1947 Thor Heyerdahl completes his *Kon-Tiki* voyage, and claims he has proved his theory about the first settlers in the South Pacific.

1953 Edmund Hillary and Sherpa Tenzing reach the summit of Everest.

1961 Yuri Gagarin is the first person in space.

1963 Valentina Tereshkova is the first woman in space.

1967 Francis Chichester becomes the first person to sail single-handed around the world from west to east.

1969 Neil Armstrong is the first man to walk on the Moon.

1973 Jacques Cousteau founds the Cousteau Society for the Protection of Ocean Life.

1982 Sir Ranulph Fiennes completes his Transglobe Expedition, using only surface transport to travel round the world from north to south, crossing both the Poles.

1985 Benedict Allen makes his first solo expedition, travelling to the mouth of the Amazon River in South America.

1992 Dr Mae Jemison becomes the first African-American woman astronaut.

1999 The blind adventurer Miles Hilton-Barber completes a 150-mile ultra-marathon through the Sahara Desert.

Glossary

anthropologist Someone who studies the beliefs and ways of life of different peoples around the world.

archaeologist Someone who studies the past, often by digging up old buildings and objects.

aviation The science and art of flying a plane.

aviator Someone who flies a plane.

biplane An early plane with two sets of wings, one above the other.

cosmonaut The Russian term for an astronaut, someone who travels in space.

ecologist Someone who studies the way in which human activity affects the Earth.

ejected Thrown out of something (such as out of a spacecraft).

endurance Putting up with something difficult or painful.

Free French A group of French people who fought against the rule of the Nazis in France during World War Two.

frostbite Damage to fingers, toes, nose or ears caused by extreme cold.

Great Depression A period in the 1930s, when many countries had financial problems and people lost a lot of money.

initiation ceremony An event held by some native peoples to mark the time when a young boy becomes a man. Initiation ceremonies often involve tests of courage.

lunar module The part of a spacecraft that lands on the surface of the Moon.

marathon A very long running race, usually of 42.195 kilometres (26 miles, 385 yards).

marine To do with the sea.

microlight A very light aircraft, with large, fabric-covered wings and a pilot compartment hanging underneath the wings.

navigate To travel in a boat or plane using maps and compasses and other instruments to guide you.

navigation manuals Books containing information, such as maps, that help pilots to navigate their vehicles.

navigation system A system that helps someone to steer a boat or a plane, by giving information about direction of travel, winds, etc.

navigator Someone who is expert at steering a boat or plane, using maps, compasses and other information.

Nazi Party The party led by Adolf Hitler who ruled Germany between 1933 and 1945.

nomadic Often moving from place to place, not settled in one spot.

officer Someone who is in charge of other people.

orbit To circle around something, such as the Earth.

pioneer To try out new things or new ways of doing something.

Soviet Union The very large country, including Russia and several other nations, that was formed in 1922 and lasted until 1991. The Soviet Union was run by a communist government that owned all the land and factories and provided for the people's needs.

speech-output navigation system A system that allows a blind person to steer a plane or boat because all the necessary information is given in speech.

submersible A craft that can travel underwater.

venomous Producing poison.

yak A type of long-haired ox.

zoology The study of animals and other creatures.

Index

Numbers in **bold** refer to pictures.